Lin.

Danny.

Sam.

"You need to exercise," said Lin.

"Why?" asked Danny.

"So you will live longer," said Lin.

Sam looked puzzled. "Too late —
I'm already undead."

Danny stared at Lin. "We know why you like football. Dogs like chasing balls."
"Are you saying I'm a dog?" asked Lin.

"Er, no," said Danny, quickly.
"Good," said Lin. "Get your
football kit and let's go!"

13

"So who are we playing?" asked Lin.

Jack pointed over at the other team.

Danny and Sam stared in horror.

"Oh, no," said Sam. "It can't be him!"

"It is," groaned Danny.

"I'm not scared of him," said Lin.

"I am," said Danny.

"And me," agreed Sam.

"Don't worry. It will be OK," said Lin.

Finally the football match ended.

"13—0 wasn't too bad," said Lin.

"At least I still have both of my legs!"
said Sam.

Clogger and his mates left. "Goodbye,
losers. I hope you're not too sore,"
he said.

Lin stared. "Clogger scared everyone
off the pitch. He hurt Beth and Jack.
Let's give him a scare."

That night Clogger was walking home.

He heard a noise.

He stopped.

"Who's there?" he asked.

Danny, Lin and Sam turned back into human form.

"Are you OK, Clogger? What's wrong?" asked Danny.

Clogger gulped. "I saw a werewolf, a demon and a zombie."

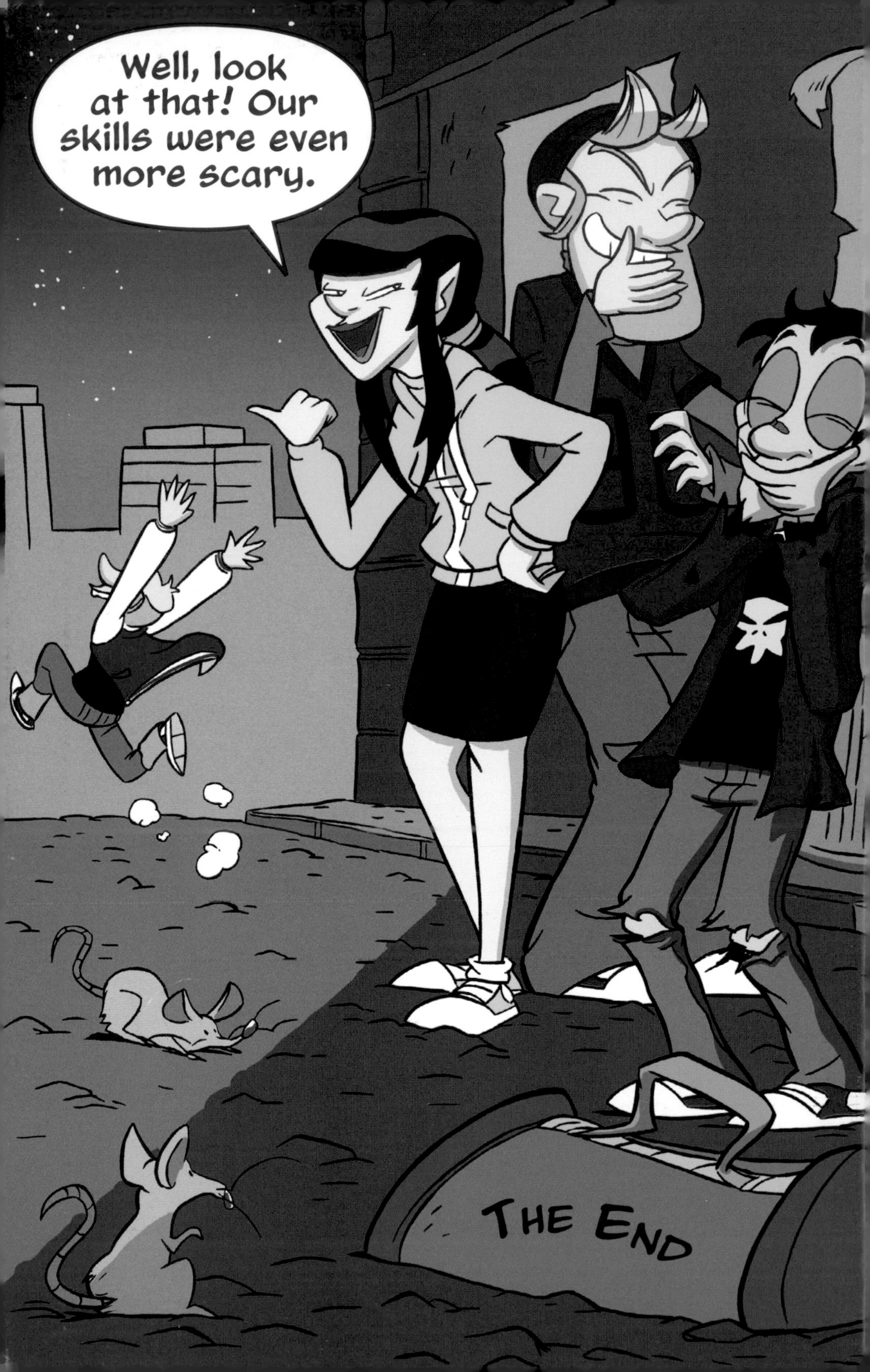
Well, look at that! Our skills were even more scary.
THE END